WITHDRAWN

L. R. COLLEGE LIBRARY CARL A. RUDISILL
LENOIR RHYNE COLLEGE

W9-ABI-539

728
M19h

101854

DATE DUE			
Aug 9 '77			
May 24 79			
May 21 '80			

WITHDRAWN
L.R. COLLEGE LIBRARY

ASPECTS OF GREEK AND ROMAN LIFE

General Editor: Professor H. H. Scullard

★ ★ ★

HOUSES, VILLAS AND PALACES IN THE ROMAN WORLD

A. G. McKay

HOUSES, VILLAS AND PALACES IN THE ROMAN WORLD

A. G. McKay

CARL A. RUDISILL LIBRARY
LENOIR RHYNE COLLEGE

CORNELL UNIVERSITY PRESS

ITHACA, NEW YORK

For
Jean,
Julie and Danae

728
M19h
101854
July 1977

© 1975 THAMES AND HUDSON

All rights reserved. Except for brief quotations in a review, this book,
or parts thereof, must not be reproduced in any form without per-
mission in writing from the publisher. For information address Cornell
University Press, 124 Roberts Place, Ithaca,
New York 14850.

This edition is not for sale in the United Kingdom and British
Commonwealth.

First published 1975

International Standard Book Number 0-8014-0948-9

Library of Congress Catalog Card Number 74-20425

PRINTED IN GREAT BRITAIN

CONTENTS

FOREWORD

MODERN ARCHAEOLOGY has made impressive advances in the recovery and study of the private buildings of Greeks and Romans of practically every time and a large variety of places. The Greek house, since Bertha Carr Rider's history was first published,[1] has come much more sharply into focus and has yielded structures which, however perishable, reflect a sense of dignity, a sensitivity to family needs, and an aesthetic sense quite compatible with the other achievements of the Greek spirit. The sweeping generalization, still repeated in some popular histories, that the Greeks sought the communal civic centre or *palaestra* or temple compound because their homes were so nondescript and unpleasant has been totally dispelled by the marvellous finds at Olynthus and Delos, and more recently in Attica and Athens itself.[2] The humble fifth-century shop-dwelling of Simon the Shoemaker, Socrates' pupil, and the *atelier* home of Mikion the Athenian sculptor, evidence an unexpected degree of utility and comfort.[3] The tradition of ancient Greek house design persists, in evolution, into the present day, often with a startling similarity of attitude to domestic life.[4] There is also a constant sense of living persons in the recovered homes of the ancient Greeks and Romans, an intimacy which transcends time and recreates a family's private travails and prosperity with uncanny detail. The reconstructed *cubiculum* of the Boscoreale Villa in the Metropolitan Museum of New York, and the splendidly reconstructed Roman house at Augst (Switzerland) are only a sample of what may be done under skilled direction and with adequate funds.[5]

60, 61

The venturesome engineering genius of Hippodamus, the Milesian town-planner, and others of the same profession who remain anonymous, revolutionized Greek city plans in fifth-century Hellas and Magna Graecia and undoubtedly sparked off